Soul Searching

**Find your answers
to your personal and professional
dilemmas or challenges.**

Managing Editor:
Denny Portier-Terpstra

Contributors:
Bettina Pickering
Norwyn Kam
Barbara J. Cormack
Steve Rogers
Dr. Charuni Senanayake
Alyson Daley
Loren Schmal
Jenny Schmal

Amarantine, Denny Portier-Terpstra, Bettina Pickering, Norwyn Kam, Barbara J. Cormack, Steve Rogers, Dr. Charuni Senanayake, Alyson Daley, Loren Schmal, and Jenny Schmal asserts their moral rights to be identified as the authors of this work.

For more information: www.Amarantine.Life

ISBN: 978-1-939556-33-2 (Print)
ISBN: 978-1-939556-34-9 (eBook)

ISSN: 2515-7434 (Online)
ISSN: 2515-7426 (Print)

First published: January, 2018 UK

Images used throughout this book are sourced from Pixabay, Dreamstime, 123RF, PresenterMedia, Shutterstock, or Alphaspirit | Dreamstime.com.

Contents

Denny's
Deliberations

by

Denny Por ier-Terpstra

As I was driving home from a trip last week, I sat in the car and I became more agitated by the minute. Visibility was horrible because it was dark and raining, it was extremely busy on the road because we were in the middle of rush hour, and all drivers seem to have gotten mad in response to the traffic jams and road works going on about every other mile. I should have been home in about 90 minutes, but I had been on the road for over 2 hrs and home was still nowhere near.

I was rather vocal about my misery, and my husband sitting next to me must have become tired of listening to my complaints, as he turned on the radio. Once he found some tunes he liked, he turned up the volume, and that was the end to our 'conversation' a.k.a. my moaning. Initially that irritated me as well. Who the heck did he think he was, shutting me off like that?!

But we weren't even half way through the first song, and my focus started to shift from being irritated about anything and everything to quietly humming along with the song. By the time we moved on to the next song, we were both singing out loud.

And as we sang, my mind started to wonder off and live a life on its own. I remembered times long gone when I had first heard the song and how I learned the lyrics as I was just a little girl (and how I actually sung the wrong words for years). I thought back about the hopes and dreams I had when I was that little girl. Had my life turned out how I then had hoped it to be when I grew up? What was different? Was it by choice or circumstances or? Do I want to change anything? How can I do that?

By the time we finally got home, about 1 hour later, I was

actually sorry that the drive was over already. I felt completely reenergised by the singing, and totally inspired by the thoughts that had crossed my mind. Without consciously setting my mind to it, I had just spent an hour of true Soul Searching, and it had cleared all dark clouds from my mood.

And the great thing is, Soul Searching can be done anywhere as and when you need it. I hope that this issue of Amarantine will inspire you to do some Soul Searching as well. And if you're not sure where to start, there are many suggestions throughout the magazine on what you could be doing to get your Soul Searcher in motion. Enjoy the ride!

Warmest regards,

Denny

Denny Portier-Terpstra
Managing Editor Amarantine

Dark night(s) of the soul

by

Bettina Pickering

Many people enter a "dark night of the soul" period at some stage in their lives.

It can be triggered by a traumatic experience such as a difficult divorce, a car accident, loss of a job, death of a loved one, or a serious health issue. It can also be triggered by a long period of sameness such as hardly any change over a good number of years. It can also be trigged by living life according to other people's standards and beliefs such as parents or the community one grew up in, and suddenly waking up to the fact that one's life was not one's own.

Dark nights of the soul are times when we question everything about our identity and our spiritual beliefs. In effect, we descend into a spiritual crisis or a deep darkness. This may manifest in putting into question one's religious beliefs, one's purpose in the world or even questioning one's sanity. It may manifest in physical symptoms such as listlessness and heaviness.

Entering into this soul-searching time can cause people to question everything about themselves. The questions are emerging from deep within rather than from conscious awareness.

These are questions such as:
- Who am I?
  Who am I really?
- What makes me happy?
- What do I want from life?
- What is my purpose?
- What am I here for to do?
- Is this it?
  Is this what my life is going to be like for the next 10, 20,

30 years?
- What else is there for me?

These are deep, deep questions. And often the answers are not immediately accessible.

In former times dark nights of the soul were recognised by religious orders and the religious afflicted by them supported by their orders. It was seen as something special and usually led to people such as St. John of the Cross or St. Saint Thérèse of Lisieux achieving much deeper connection to their faith.

This soul-searching period can be accompanied by a deep sadness or depression for some people, which shrouds the self-discovery process in a negative, dark mist. They often miss the opportunity to explore who they really are, as their focus is consumed by how they feel (or not feel) physically, mentally and emotionally.

Today, dark nights of soul are sometimes confused with depression, burnout and results of an illness. We fear the darkness, the not knowing, the uncertainty. We also don't have time to honour the process. And, when it happens, we often don't have the sympathetic support system the religious of old had around them. Thus, in today's world, some people turn to alcohol, thrill seeking or medication to eliminate dark of the soul symptoms.

I have been through at least three major, prolonged periods of dark nights of the soul that were triggered by a severe illness, a car accident and an identity crisis. I have also been through one positive soul-searching period that was triggered by falling in love. All dark nights of the soul or spiritual crises had a number of things in common.

What I want to share is my learning that I took from these periods of spiritual crisis and renewal.

The first dark night of the soul, I didn't recognise as such. I was very ill with a strange, virulent flu that would not shift. It was so debilitating that I lost a huge amount of weight and for months after I could not bear to eat certain foods. However, this was not the worst part. What was really terrifying about this illness was that my life appeared completely futile. There seemed to be no point to go on if things remained the same: Finish A levels, go to Uni, study something, get a job for life, retire, get a pension and die. What was the point of that?

Questions just emerged from deep inside. Questions I could not answer and not see an answer to. My parents did not understand. When I shared some of my questions they came back with platitudes but no real answers. They had never questioned their beliefs, their life or their identity and did not recognise what was going on for me. I felt alone, misunderstood and not taken seriously.

I remember that during the worst time of the illness, I was drawn to a book which turned out to be my one glimmer of hope. I had bought it on a whim as young girl of 13 but never read it: The Dark Soul, by Liam O'Flaherty. In this book, a priest experiences his own dark night of the soul and finds healing and answers in the sea.

It was a revelation.

I was not alone.

My key learnings at the time were:
- **You are not alone.** Today there are many books and

resources that describe dark nights of the soul and how to navigate them.

- **You have the power to change your life** by taking action. Dark nights of the soul respond to one taking some sort of positive action. Reaching out, reading a book, focussing on small rays of positive experiences.
- **Dark nights of the soul have an end** and with that end comes incredible clarity, new energy and new depth of connection.

This dark night of the soul showed me my path. Finish school early, study something universal like engineering, relocate to the UK and study for an MBA. I got crystal clear about what I wanted and needed at this stage in my life.

The second dark night of the soul was induced by a car accident in December 2005. The other party claimed the accident was my fault, although it clearly was not. It took almost a year to get through the legalities before I received compensation. The pain resulting from the accident did not shift within 2 weeks as the doctor I saw on the day of the accident told me. It just got worse, and the pain lasted for over a year. Accompanying the pain was a constant feeling of being lost, alone, fighting a losing battle, tired and dizzy, and an almost all-consuming sadness. Many times, I wondered what would happen, if I just let myself drop somewhere and not ever get up again.

Questions arose deep from my innermost self as to what my purpose was, what meaning my life had and what the point of my job was. Suffice it to say, I worked throughout the year, had many unpleasant experiences that appeared as if the world had it in for me at a time when I would have needed support the most.

However, there are a number of things that I learnt during that year:

- **Be clear as to what you need.** What you need might be the bigger picture, not the immediate detail. Ask for what you need of yourself and others, clearly.
- **Slow down.** Do what you can and acknowledge yourself for the smallest successes. Say no 80% more than you say yes.
- **Receive support, trust and help as gifts.** Don't expect them and when they come, celebrate them, witness them, cherish them.
- **Ask for miracles, i.e. suspend disbelief.** Whilst this sounds strange, it works. I won a Ryanair flight that period and met my soul mate.

This time around, I took from it, that my path would take me to learn Qi Gong which had healed the injuries from the car accident and get independent of traditional western health practitioners.

The third dark night of the soul was really a bright day of the soul. My time with my soulmate was magical, expansive and felt like a fairy tale at times. My awareness was so heightened I noticed things I would have never recognised. I started to do Shamanic walking; a method to use a mindful walk in nature or a city to get answers to your innermost questions. My energetic abilities expanded, I became a Qi Gong teacher several times over, improved my eye sight significantly, left employment, set up my company, and trained to become a professional coach.

The fourth dark night of the soul was triggered by the breakup with my soulmate, the love of my life. Whilst we still loved each other and probably always will, unfortunately our paths took us in different directions. Making the choice to let him go was the most devastating decision I ever had to make. I cried almost every day for a long time. Other negative things happened on top of that which I felt unequal to deal with and which made the whole experience even worse. I again felt that pointlessness, the devastating darkness of: "What's the point?". The whole period was so dark, that I could not coach anyone, almost lost my business, my home and got into significant debt. I lost friendships and even business partners as I was in no state to give anything to anyone, neither was I able to attract the amount of business that I needed. The worst was, I could not even articulate what was going on in words that would make sense to another human being. I could not even ask for help in ways that others understood, as every time I did, all I got was platitudes and unhelpful advice. What I needed instead was witnesses, space holders, clarity distillers.

This time though, I had all the learnings from my previous dark and bright days of the soul episodes.

It seems the unconscious takes those times where we are most vulnerable, hurt and hurting, as an open invitation to help us grow and discover who we can become. You cannot rush the unconscious, be attached to specific answers, or even, to getting answers.

This period gave me the following learnings:
- Honour the process and allow answers to emerge. Don't fight it, judge it or judge yourself. It takes as long as it takes. Take every day as a new beginning, honour what you are going through. For me that started lifting the clouds.

- Make an effort to find a good coach or mentor who has been through something similar. People like that can hold space, and create space with you, so the answers to your unspoken questions can emerge.
- **Your answers come in different guises.** For example, I discovered a deeply transformative process, I call change weaving, in this period. It is rooted in Celtic wisdom, and elements of it are described in an ancient Celtic text. This process came to me when I visited Tara, the ancient seat of the Irish high kings in the summer of 2014. Because I was so raw, hurt and open, Tara's energies were able to reach me easily and show me the process.

  I went through the process I discovered many times over. It cleared so much darkness, limiting beliefs and helped me understand what I truly wanted. It also created a platform for me to transform.

This time around, I became a published author, had my most profitable years in business yet, paid off my mortgage, was able to understand at least one of my purposes[1] and was able to bring unconditional love back into my life in the form of two amazing rescue cats, Paddy and Seamus. I also acquired deeper energetic abilities and my coaching expanded into helping people overcome trauma.

Each period of soul-searching is expansive, that is the nature of the questions that come up from deep inside. Whilst dark nights of the soul or soul-searching episodes can be devastating, deeply unsettling, exhausting and filled with despair, they can also be miraculous, magical and

---

[1] I don't believe that we can only have one purpose in life. Like we can have several careers, we can have several purposes.

incredibly energising. Each of them has their own gifts and if used well they provide a growth spurt in one's development. Each allowed me to expand beyond what I thought was possible for me, each took me where I needed to go.

One thing I would say, when a soul-searching episode is triggered, go inside first. Take things slowly, rather than rushing after a cure or help. Make sure you are clear about what you need first and foremost, and do not solely rely on what others believe you need. When you are clear look for people with similar experiences and learn from them.

Always check back with yourself. You are stronger[2] than you think and all soul-searching episodes, dark or light, serve a purpose and will provide answers and learnings, if one is open to that. Your soul will never put you through something you cannot deal with.

Bettina Pickering
© 2018 Bettina Pickering

Bettina Pickering is a transformative leadership coach, entrepreneur mentor, business transformation and change consultant, author and speaker.

---

[2] I was fortunate to get through the dark episodes without any other medication than ibuprofen (which I took throughout one for the physical pain). I know others who benefited from anti-depressive medication during the dark periods. If this is you, don't ever judge yourself. You need what you need. However, make sure to use that period to take the learnings and ask for answers gently. Don't just exist through these periods without taking advantage of what they have to offer to you.

Stop thinking, Start doing!

So, you are shifting through this book and you realise that all this deep thinking stuff really isn't for you? Maybe you're more into doing than thinking? Or maybe you feel you simply need a break from thinking all the time? But still, you have all these unanswered life questions, and you want to find some answers...

There is good news! Soul Searching is usually associated with hard thinking, but it can (and will) also happen when we do exactly the opposite: not thinking at all.

Not thinking, even if only for a minute, is however a real challenge. Every waking moment, thoughts will flow in and out of our minds all the time. Just whilst writing these few sentences, various thoughts have crossed my mind. I remembered that I still have to decide on what we have for dinner this evening and I wondered what the time was, I noticed that my plants need water, I wondered why a European Robin was landing on my window, and I remarked that the neighbour who just passed by that same window was wearing very nice shoes. Our thoughts will go on and on, and it's very hard to shut them off. In Bhuddism, they call this constant stream of thoughts "discursive thinking".

Of course, we are thinking beings for a reason, and our capacity to think is exactly what helps us move through life. But have you ever consciously given your mind a break and tried to stop that constant flow of thoughts? We do give our bodies a rest every time that we go to sleep, but even when we are asleep our minds will continue to be busy and process all the thoughts that we didn't get to during the day (which is why we dream).

However, like our bodies, our minds need a rest every now and then, to allow us to "wake up" feeling better, reenergised, and see the world (and our problems) with a refreshed sense of clarity and positivity.

The most obvious way to rest your mind is, of course, by meditation. It may take you some time to learn how to do it, but most practitioners will tell you that meditation can and will be both healing and inspiring. Scientific research even shows that meditation can help treat a variety of physical and mental conditions too (although most also recognise that further research is needed to fully understand the workings and effects of meditation). But what if meditation isn't your thing either?

Well, what meditation actually does, is helping your mind to relax and stop that constant stream of thoughts, by focussing on just one thing. This "one thing" could be an object, or your breathing, or basically anything. As we know, our minds will soon wonder off to other things anyway (eg what's for dinner, what's the time, etc), but with meditation you just observe that you have these thoughts, and you don't respond to them (eg, you don't start your shopping list, you don't watch your clock, etc.). All you do, is recognise that the thought is there, and then return your focus to whatever it was that you were focussing on.

When you don't want to meditate, there may be other things that can help you to focus your mind on just one thing, and stop it from wondering off in all other directions. Many people report that exercise or sports will do the trick for them, and for others it may be reading a book, working on arts and crafts, making music, or taking a long shower. If you haven't found what stops your thoughts yet, just try out a few things and evaluate how your mind responded to it. And once you've found "your thing", make sure to fit it into your schedule regularly (preferably daily), and give your mind that well needed break to ultimate help you think quicker and better.

"F.E.A.R.
has two meanings:
Forget everything and run
or
face everything and rise.
The choice is yours."
Zig Ziglar

"The Soul Always Knows
What to Do to Heal Itself.
The Challenge is to
Silence the Mind."
Caroline Myss

"Quiet the mind,
and the soul will speak."
Ma Jaya Sati Bhagavati

**"And,
when you want something,
all the universe conspires
in helping you to achieve it."**
Paulo Coelho, The Alchemist

**"Be the change
that you wish
to see
in the world."**
Mahatma Gandhi

**"Look for something positive
in every day,
even if some days
you have to look
a little harder."**
ANON

Meet the Captain of the Directionless Ship

by
Norwyn Kam

. . . . You!

Now wait a minute, you weren't expecting that you were going to be the main attraction to this show, I'll bet. However, here's a bold claim that I have about you. You, my friend, are a captain of a directionless ship right now. Now before those eyebrows frown and you get that quizzical look on your face, let's bring some perspective to this. My claim may be bold, but I can tell you it's one that has great odds. How can I be so sure, you ask? Well, I'm about to ask you a question that I want you to answer honestly. Don't worry, nobody is looking so don't hold back on this one. Here it is...

"WHAT'S YOUR PURPOSE IN LIFE?"

Now give your brain a break and stop trying to search the vast corners of your consciousness for an answer. If you weren't able to come up with the answer to that question in the first four seconds of reading that question, then I think we can safely say that you may not have found your purpose in life yet. But here's the thing; That's perfectly okay.

This year has brought about many great things, one of them being the rise in interest of a spiritual awakening of sorts. Each day while browsing various social media platforms it becomes apparent that more people are taking the task of finding purpose and direction seriously, even if just to post a pic of them doing a yoga pose with a motivational caption about the intricacies of life (we all know those people). But I think that this is a good thing, for it's a direction worth moving towards. Anyone who tells me that they are spiritual or spiritually inclined draws a huge smile on my face, not because there's anything socially more appealing or better for those who are on a spiritual journey opposed to those who aren't. But what gets me excited is in the knowingness that those who are more "spiritual" are often more "self-aware", and that, my friends, is everything.

I am the biggest supporter of self-awareness because I believe wholeheartedly that just having that one thing, can lead you to a much happier and fulfilled life. No complicated university degree or corporate MBA needed here, just pure self-awareness. A thing that can be attained by anyone, and the best part it is that it lives within all of us. All we need to do is find the unlocks that will help us uncover this goldmine that we're sitting on. Let's go back to our question of the day: "What's your purpose in life?" Admittedly, that's a tough question to answer as we've discovered, but I believe there's a reason for that. Because it doesn't exist!

Hooooooooold on, let me explain and share my perspective on that. I am not for one second saying that purpose doesn't exist, however, what I am saying is that the context in which we understand that question is wrong, and I think it's causing a lot of us to lean our ladders against the wrong wall. When we think about purpose, we almost immediately think of this incredibly far-fetched idea, where we need to find the next cure for cancer or heroically save the world or something else profound. If this is your preconceived idea of purpose, then I implore you to take that idea, put it in a box and throw that MF in the ocean with a large anchor to keep it down forever. Because that is not purpose!

I believe that finding one's purpose should never be this daunting journey that almost seems unreachable. How would we ever achieve something that we don't even believe that we can, deep down? The short answer is that we won't ever be able to, so don't bother trying. The other thing I want you to understand is that "purpose" in the context that we understand it is wrong. Not the actual purpose, but the context is the culprit here. Most people look at purpose as a single fixed point in time, something that has a very specific time, place and meaning. Think of a company like Apple. We all know the Apple purpose, and hopefully, you all know the purpose of the company you are working for right now (yes, I am looking at you). But you see, that works fine for a one-dimensioned entity like a company and organization. But you are not a one-dimensional entity; you are far from that. You are a kaleidoscopic mess of beauty, energy, atoms, miracles, and magic. Your humanity is far more complex than any brick building with a name on it. You are diverse, and your journey is boundless, and through this journey of your life, you will experience many different things, the good, the bad and downright chaotic. But that's why you are such a beautiful being, because you can experience so many different things in your time here, all varying from the other 6 billion plus people on this planet right now.

When you think of how unique you are, do you think that you were meant to have only ONE singular purpose throughout your entire life? I don't think so. Far from it, in fact. And that is my point. Every single one of us, I believe, can and will have multiple "purposes" in the course of our lifetime. We were never programmed to follow a set structure of beliefs and ideals. If that was the case, I can guarantee you that space travel would have never happened, because who would have been taught to have a purpose of traveling into an unknown frontier like space one day? It was a purpose that was created by the individual, and it can be decided and changed at any time of our lives. You may have a purpose in your life right now, but that doesn't have to be your ONLY purpose in life. You can have many different purposes, and they can be changed as your journey changes. One of the greatest gifts I have learned is that you should never become so attached to a specific outcome that you lose sight of the possibility that there's another path that could lead you to the same place. I for one have many purposes, and some of them are small-scale, some are larger. They are different from goals, in a sense that they are not tangible things to attain but more of having a deeper understanding for why you want it. Having a double story mansion is a goal, but what's the purpose of why you want it? That is an example of a small scale purpose. Larger scale purpose is all about lasting impact, or so it is in my eyes. Here you have to play for legacy, for long-term memory and for the thing that you want to be remembered for.

The fact remains that it's up to you, and always has been up to you. You get to decide what you want your purpose to be and that could be anything. As long as you come to that decision void from any external influences from family or friends. This needs to be your decision and yours alone; this is where self-awareness comes in. When you know what makes you happy and you're living life on your terms being a total savage, then you are also more inclined to decide and find a purpose that you choose. Once you have, all you need to do is make sure you are tracking towards that image and enjoy the incredible journey. It doesn't matter how far or close you get to it, what does matter is that you are forging your own path for your life. That leads to levels of joy and fulfilment that so many never find. So my wish for you is to take control of the ship you are captaining right now and find your island. Once you have decided where your island is, then move towards it every day, endure the stormy seas and keep going until the shores of your purpose reach you. Once you have planted your flag on the island, reset and search for your next island adventure for that is a great life, worth living. Just whatever you do, promise me that you will never become a captain of a directionless ship. You owe it to yourself to find happiness and slay this life.

Norwyn Kam
© 2018 Norwyn Kam

Wake Pray Slay
Slaying an Unfulfilled Existence

Your Soul Searching Wheel

Step-by-Step Series

by
Barbara J. Cormack

We all talk about soul searching, but do we do it?

Soul Searching is all about reaching inside and recognising those inner most secrets. Often those inner most secrets are kept hidden because of the focus. The day-to-day focus of life keeps each one of us extremely busy.

Your Soul Searching Wheel is a process that not only helps you identify what you want from your life, but also helps you explore your reasons. This process is based on a Life Coaching tool, which is used at the beginning of the range of tools and techniques used by Coaches; called the Wheel of Life.

The Wheel of Life is simply used to represent a helicopter view of how balanced your life is today, through understanding the segments of your life as it is today. The segments are simply a way of describing each element of your life. The reason it is called a 'wheel' is because it is visually represented as a wheel. The spokes of the wheel represent the different segments.

Although the segments of your Wheel will change over time as you move through the different phases of your life, when you are looking at your Soul Searching Wheel today; it is important that you look at your life as it is today.

Your Wheel of Life may include segments like your health, your environment, your professional life (career or business), your wealth (and this may not only refer to money and finances), your growth (personal and professional growth), your significant other (boy/girl-friend, partner, husband/wife), your family, your friends, your colleagues, your hobbies, your interests, your fun, your travelling/holidays, and the list goes on. Your Wheel should include every element of your life as it is today.

This article will show an example Wheel as well as providing you with a blank Wheel to create your own. It is important that you do create your own Wheel and not use one that someone else has created for you. This will allow you to start your soul searching process.

As a Life Coach, this is an exercise that we would recommend that you do regularly. Regularly has no definition and simply means that you can do this exercise when you have a need to understand how balanced your life is, and to help you identify any specific segments that need to be focused on.

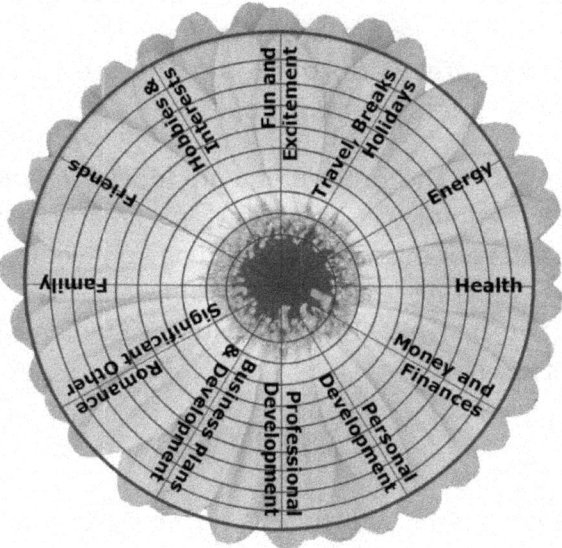

"Death is not the greatest loss in life.
The greatest loss is
what dies inside us while we live."
Norman Cousins

Your Soul Searching Wheel will help you understand, revive and recognise what is in your inner most soul, your inner most secrets.

It is important that you have no interruptions while you work through this process.

STEP ONE

Taking your life **as it is today**, write down all the areas of importance in your life. There may be some areas that you feel are not important; write these down too. It is only by going through this process and the steps in the following issues; that will help you understand and identify which areas are important. There is no right and there is no wrong when you define the areas in your life – whatever you decide the areas are, these are the areas you want to identify as the segments in your life.

Remember in this process you are looking at your life **as it is today.** Where you write down an area or segment that relates to your past, or is something you would like in your future; separate these into a different list. Today it is important that you only work with the elements of your life **as it is today**.

STEP TWO

There is no right and there is no wrong to the number of segments you have in your life, although I would caution you to group like elements together e.g. 'health' could incorporate 'physical fitness', 'fitness', 'optimum health'. Once you have your list, look through it and see how many of your segments are similar and group them together.

STEP THREE

Now draw yourself a circle with 10 rings. These rings are used to identify the levels of satisfaction in your life, with the in the centre representing 0 (low) and each ring increasing to 10, the outer ring (high). Now add the spokes, which are used to identify the segments of your life. You need to add 1 spoke for each segment on your summarised list from step two above. This example Wheel has 12 segments, but your circle must have as many or as few as you have defined in your life today.

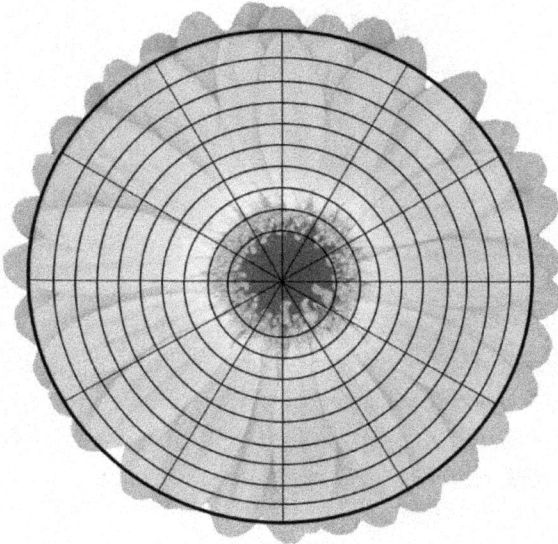

STEP FOUR

Once you have drawn your Wheel of Life, enter onto it all your OWN segments for your life as your life **as is today**. Don't enter segments that are not in your life today; segments from your past, or those you want to bring into your future.

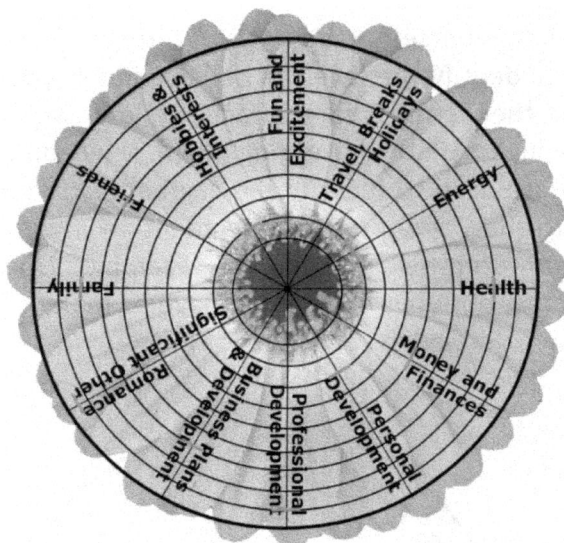

Before you continue with the remaining steps, clear your mind of all your current thoughts – work, spouse/partner, children, friends, customers, or anything else. Turn off your mobile! Make sure that any other method of communication is closed down. Let those around you know that you need time with no disturbances or interruptions to work through this process. It is important that you have no interruptions while you work on your own soul searching.

STEP FIVE

Taking your completed Soul Searching Wheel, without thinking or taking time to think, draw on each spoke of your wheel your own levels of satisfaction in each segment of your life **as your life is today** and not as you would like your life to be (like the example below).

To really make a success of your own soul searching, it is important that you are drawing in the levels of satisfaction in your life **as it is today**, without stopping to think about or analyse what you are drawing. Analysing, think, or assessing your thoughts at this time can produce inaccurate results. (And don't worry if you feel you must analyse, as we'll get to do it later on in this process).

To draw in your level of satisfaction in each segment, just draw a straight or slightly curved line across the spoke of each segment of the wheel. The centre of the wheel represents 0 or a low satisfaction in your life; and the outer rim represents 10 or a high satisfaction in your life). Therefore, where a segment of your life is to be represented as low satisfaction, draw it closer to the centre of the wheel; and where an area is represented as high satisfaction, draw it closer to the outer rim of the wheel.

Take for example, one segment of your life, like 'career'. Do you have any career plans? What career plans have you got? When did you last look at your career plans? When did you last think about your career? Have you just got career dreams? Or aspirations? Or just thoughts? When did you last sit down and think about your career? Do your thoughts, plans, aspirations, dreams, or goals meet your inner most career desires?

If you look at your Soul Searching Wheel of Life and take the centre of wheel as '0' which represents the low areas in your life, and the outer ring as '10' to represent the high areas of your life; NOW rank each segment of your life as it is TODAY!

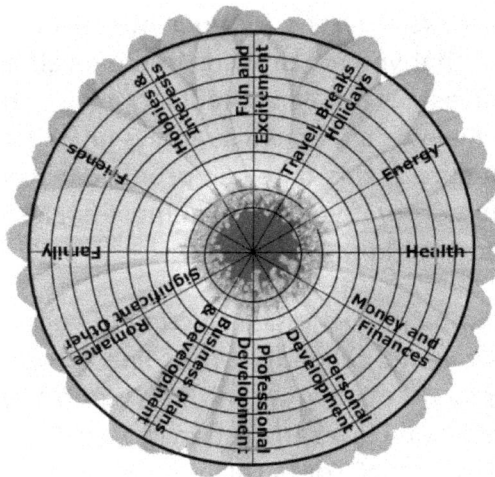

STEP SIX

After ranking each segment of your life, join up these lines. This will visually demonstrate the reason that this is called a 'wheel'. Once you have joined up the lines, you have created your own new outer rim of your own Soul Searching Wheel of Life.

Does your Wheel of Life look something like this one?

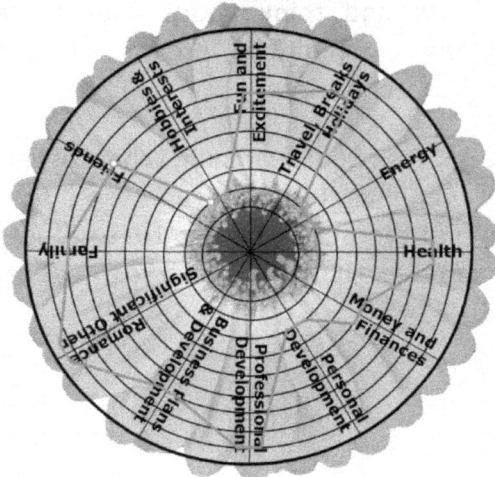

If you take the grey line as your own Soul Searching Wheel of Life rim, what would it be like if you started to drive your car with a wheel of this shape?

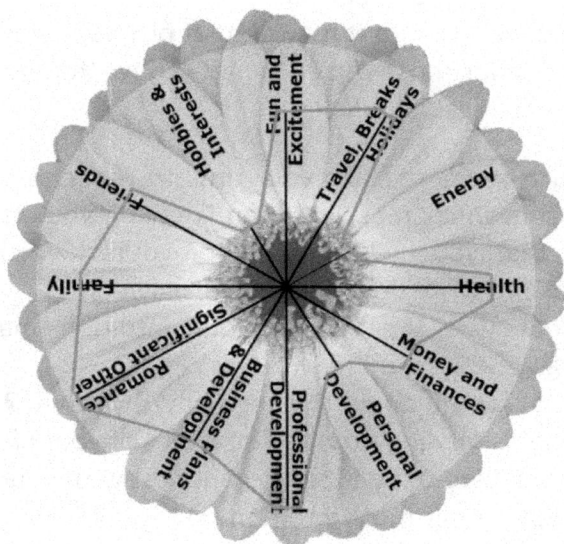

Uncomfortable ... uneven ... in many ways dangerous.

The Life Coaching exercise around the Wheel of Life gives you two areas to consider. The first is the 'balance' in your life; and the second is the 'satisfaction' you have in each segment.

'Balanced' doesn't mean that each segment of your life has to be set to '10'. A life where all the segments are found, for example to be between 7 and 8, shows a life that is more evenly balanced.

STEP SEVEN

Take one segment at a time. It doesn't matter which

segment you start with, but I always suggest that you allow your inner most intuition to guide you to the first segment you want to start with. Sometimes this will be the one segment that you feel has been ignored in past weeks, months, or years; or it may be that one segment that you - in your inner most secret being - know that you want to make a change.

For each segment, take your time to reflect and consider what your inner most intuition is telling you. In the quiet space that you have created for yourself, pick up your journal and write down your own answers:

1. What was the reason your intuition marked this segment of your life with this result?
2. What is right about this segment of your life?
3. What is missing from this segment of your life?
4. If you were to be absolutely honest with yourself, what is your inner most intuition telling you that you desire from this segment of your life? Sometimes this question may feel a little scary; because you may now need to admit to yourself that what you want is what you don't have now. It may be that you will make a change in your life that someone else or others may not like. Don't be influenced by anyone else. If you can't design the life you want to live, who will?
5. Who is involved with you in this segment of your life?
6. Who is missing from this segment of your life? This person may be someone you don't know yet; but know the type and characteristics of the person you want in your life – write down all the details.
7. Who is in this segment of your life that you don't want to remain?
8. What else do you want to consider in this segment of your life? It may be the environment, or a choice you

made that hasn't resulted in what you expected, or anything else.

"We have, each of us,
a life story, whose continuity,
whose sense, is our lives."
Oliver Sacks

STEP EIGHT

Once you have gone through each segment, identify the three most important segments that you, in your inner most heart, want to change.

Remember that Soul Searching is all about reaching inside and recognising those inner most secrets; often those inner most secrets that are kept hidden because of the focus as the day-to-day focus of life keeps you extremely busy.

Taking the first of the three segments that you have selected, on a clean page in your journal:
1. My inner most dream or aspiration for this segment is ...
2. What do I have in this segment right now, that meets my inner most dream?
3. What do I not have in this segment right now to meet my inner most dream?
4. To be living the life of my dream or aspiration, what do I need to change?

STEP NINE

Reflect on what you have written down for each segment in step eight, and on a clean sheet of paper in your journal; write down in a short sentence what your inner most heart wants in your life for this segment.

In the next issue we will progress changing your life step-by-step and talk about one of the secrets to achieving your inner most dreams, learning to say 'NO' to what you don't want and 'YES' to what you do want.

Barbara J. Cormack
© 2018 Barbara J. Cormack

Barbara J. Cormack AFC, AFM, MNMC is an award winning coach, an author, mentor, trainer, and a sought after international speaker.

No one told you when to run, you missed the starting gun

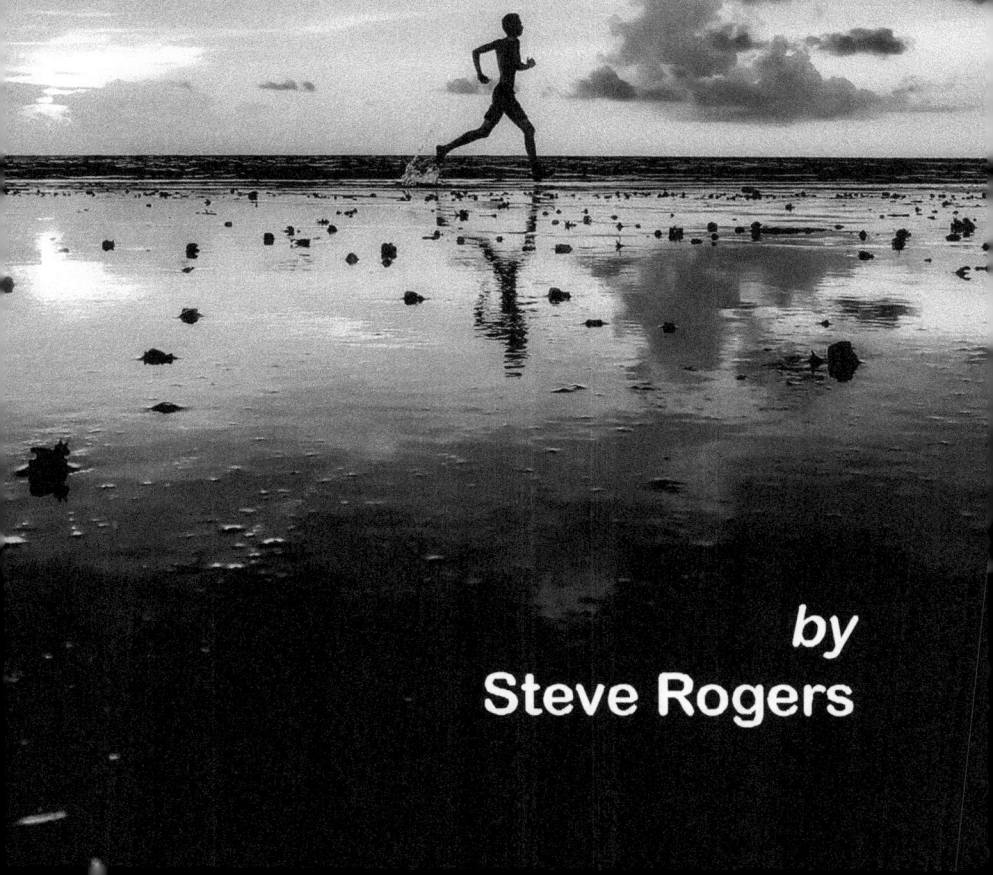

by
Steve Rogers

No one told you when to run, you missed the starting gun ...[3]

There are 3 levels of Searching:

Level 1: Mundane:

If we ask ourselves on a Friday: "What should I do this weekend?"; the options are endless and comfortable. Read a book, shopping, voluntary work, movies, housework, homework, gardening, DIY, a second job for extra income, banking, budgeting, sport, sleeping, accepting invitations to friends and family, inviting friends and family to visit etc.

Easy.

Level 2: Dig a little deeper:

"I need to change/improve/develop". This requires more thought, possibly pen and paper, quiet time, reflection. We might conclude such episodes with resolutions to lose weight, stop smoking, change jobs, take a holiday, dump the partner, move home/suburb/city/country.

A lot of the reflection involved at Level 2 is about the current situation and how it could be better. I am unfit, I would like to get fit. The getting fit uses known regimes. I used to belong to the gym, I must re-join the gym. I used to be 50/60/70/80 kgs, Now, I'm 60/70/80/90 kgs. I must go back to where I was.

I am unhappily employed, I'd like a better job. Probably in a

---

[3] *Lyrics from the song 'Time' by Mason, Waters, Wright, Gilmour off the album 'The Dark Side of The Moon'*

similar company doing similar work in a similar town.

I am unhappy in my relationship: he or she doesn't make me happy. i.e. it's not my fault, it's them. It's my boss, it's my job. But it's not _me_.

Level 3: Me:

Soul searching is about a much deeper level of introspection. It questions our very existence. It begs a review of our lives to date and the journey to now. It asks a better question: how successfully have I built my own life to be what it could be? What have I done for myself, my friends, partners, colleagues, parents, children, siblings, suppliers, clients, strangers. Not to mention animals, plants, belongings, assets, liabilities, expenses, choices, mistakes. And successes, good deeds, smart moves, simple giving.

That's a lot to unpack.

Soul searching is not a quick fix. We very rarely make the time for soul searching. Life is too busy. We have bills to pay, targets to reach, parties to join, sport to play, movies to watch, chores to do …

"How am I supposed to make time to search my soul!?"

Herein lies the rub. Most people are stuck on the rollercoaster of life with its natural highs and lows. The highs aren't that high but the lows aren't that low either.

As Pink Floyd famously sang in that seminal hymn about time:

> _Ticking away the moments_
> _that make up a dull day_

You fritter and waste the hours
in an offhand way.
Kicking around on a piece of ground
in your home town
Waiting for someone or something
to show you the way.

Tired of lying in the sunshine
staying home to watch the rain.
You are young and life is long and there is time to kill
today.
And then one day you find
ten years have got behind you.
No one told you when to run,
you missed the starting gun.

So you run and you run
to catch up with the sun
but it's sinking
Racing around to come up
behind you again.
The sun is the same in a relative way
but you're older,
Shorter of breath and
one day closer to death.

Every year is getting shorter
never seem to find the time.
Plans that either come to naught
or half a page of scribbled lines
Hanging on in quiet desperation
is the English way
The time is gone, the song is over,

Thought I'd something more to say [4]

The key line in the song to me is: *"You are young and life is long and there is time to kill today."*

I like to count myself as mentally young but physically, well …, less young! I can remember sitting in junior school watching the classroom clock. There were 5 minutes to go and that seemed like an eternity. At high school, 2 weeks was a long time. Today, a month feels like the 5 minutes I grimaced at in junior school! There's no doubt that the clock appears to run faster as we age. In my twenties and thirties, I don't remember thinking how quickly the years roll past. Today, I'm amazed that another year is starting. Again.

So when you're young and your life is largely ahead of you, you feel as if you have time to kill. It's only when the time is past and the sun is sinking to come up behind you again, that you realise **time is now in charge**, no longer you.

And if you're too busy to stop the clock, it runs faster still.

Until you stop the clock and search your soul. Until you get off the rollercoaster, stand steady and still and look at the movie of your life. Until you take the time to sit, reflect, think, write and question your raison d'être, the clock will win the war for control.

Why?

If we don't know where we're going, we have no feeling for progress. If I choose today to visit a friend who takes my energy. If I choose to read a book with no link to my being.

---

[4] https://en.wikipedia.org/wiki/The_7_Habits_of_Highly_Effective_People

If I choose to do something simply because it's in front of me. I lose time. A lot of time without progress on the journey through our short lives on this mortal coil.

And when month end comes, we moan about the mundane. Politics, movie star antics, crime, fashion, food, the score line for our favourite team from our favourite sport and the neighbour's bad manners. I'm guilty as charged. As Robert Mugabe's vicious reign was coming to an end after 37 long years, I've read many articles about it. But really, does it matter? Can I influence events in another country?

Can I influence events in my own home? That might be a better use of my time today!

In my last article for Amarantine, about prioritising self-development, I wrote that we should identify a piece of time each week that we dedicate to our self-development.

Soul searching requires the same time but at a deeper level. Soul searching is about your epitaph. If we begin with the end in mind as Stephen Covey implored us to do in 1988[2], we have to visit today from the future.

The simple things are easy: how many children should I have, how much money would I like to earn, which friends should I choose, what sports/hobbies should I have, what books should I read. Easy.

But my *epitaph*? I must write today what I want written about me in 10, 20, 30, 40, 50 years' time!?

Harder. Soul searching.

Most people are so busy existing, they haven't got time to

live.

Besides, if I told my husband / wife / friend / brother / sister / mother / father that I was going to search my soul, you can imagine the wise cracks: "You left your car keys there?! Ha de ha de ha!".

It's naf to search but maybe it's fear that drives us to mock anything spiritual. Maybe we fear what a truly good search of our souls might reveal.

It's bound to be critical of our choices. It's bound to ask why we took that job, why we married that girl/boy, why we walked away from opportunity X, why we pay lip service to our values but scream at our favourite sports team?

But if we don't bother to search because our lives are ahead of us and 65 is soooo far away, the sun will come up behind us and we'll be "shorter of breath and one day closer to death".

Steve Rogers
© 2017 Steve Rogers

Steve Rogers works with committed and hands on leaders and managers; and assists them to put the right people in the right jobs.

Soul Searching

Not so long ago I had a conversation with a friend whom is going through a difficult time at home and he used this exact sentence to finish off our conversation: "*I have got a lot of soul searching to do, I feel that my wife and I are so different and we have grown apart so much, that I need to make some kind of change or decision about our future*".

This is a fairly profound statement and I felt I really need to understand why people need to do Soul Searching. A soul is one's self, your being, it's what makes us human. Why then would we need to search for it? Can you even lose your soul? I have obviously watched too many movies and listened to too many stories about good and evil fighting for the souls of the dead; a certain song comes to mind about a card game between God and the Devil for the souls of the dead. However still what is soul searching?

I belief that our soul is what really makes you think about life, your memories and your findings, and how the mind and your being fit into all of the everyday things we experience.

But is that correct?

The search for the soul has been an ongoing and extensive search for centuries, in which philosophers, scientists, and doctors have all looked at this question, each from their own perspective. Dr Brian Dolan, Ph.D., researched this subject and wrote about this in his publication *"Soul searching: a brief history of the mind/body debate in the neurosciences"* (Neurosurg

Focus 23 (1):E2, 2007). He explains that neurologists may look at the brain as "the seat of the soul", and that these days they are even able to pinpoint exactly where in the brain the "soul" is seated; e.g. where in the brain our capacities to memorise, think, reflect, feel, etc. are located. Aristotle didn't look at the brain as the seat of the soul, but instead he appeared to have felt that the entire body was an instrument of the soul. Pythagoras on the other hand did believe that the brain served as the organ for the mind and the temple of the soul. And yet other philosophers linked the soul to other organs, such as the heart. And even today, there are still some cardiologists and even entire cultures who believe that the heart is instrumental to the soul. Most recently, other researchers have claimed that our soul may link with the nerve system, or can simply be found in our molecules or DNA. And as the search for our souls will probably continue for centuries to come, some scientists have concluded that the existence of the soul isn't even relevant at all.

However, when we speak of "soul searching", we usually don't take that to literally, and instead refer to our internal process of finding truth within ourselves.

We all seem to do some soul searching at one point in time, and it can be brought on by various things happening. It seems to be usually when somebody experiences some kind of setback or tragedy, or when you have problems that have to be faced, and you just don't know how to handle them. People all do soul searching in different ways and with different outcomes. We, as human beings, although very complex can be very simple as well, and we tend to make our problems much bigger than what they really are. In most cases, taking a step back and really removing yourself out of the equation, lets you see the whole picture from a different angle. This allows you to manage the problem in a holistic way, maybe even manage the external influences that were making it so difficult to see the solution.

I think, trying to make sense of the soul and doing soul searching you need to look at what and who people see as soul searchers, and if people have ever done any soul searching. Although I do feel that everybody has or will do some soul searching at least once in their lives, I think most of the time doing soul searching is not a conscious decision. It's more of an unconscious process that just happens, and then slowly but surely moves into your conscious being.

Self-proclaimed soul searchers come in many forms, but seem to often be linked to the more spiritual side of life, like shamans, tea leaf readers, regressionists, yoga teachers or masters, physics, mystics, artists, healers or astrologers to name a few.

When researching the subject of soul searching, I came across a blog by Emma Mildon where she states that, after travelling the globe looking for the answers and meeting all of the soul searchers mentioned above:

"What did I learn?

I learned that while I had emptied my bank account traveling the globe on a search for self-discovery, that actually, all the answers were deep within me — go figure!"

Profound? Maybe. But I think some of us might say that we always knew that the answers are inside us, and that we don't have to travel the world to see them. I therefore think that the real questions are: *Are you willing to look inside yourself, or are you scared of what you might find? How many of us hide the real "them" from the world, and even from themselves? Isn't "Soul Searching" finding out who you really are, and then when you do, to make the spiritual journey to see if you want to expose yourself to the world?*

Walter Shelver
© 2018 Walter Shelver

Communication Technologies

54

Soul Searching helps you to live your BEST Life ...

... don't be afraid!

by
Charuni Senanayake

When I searched for definitions of Soul Searching I found the following in a few dictionaries.

In Merriam-Webster dictionary:
"Examination of one's conscience especially with regard to motives and values".

In Urban dictionary:
"Self-analysis of our own motive or attitude toward something. Looking deep within ourselves to find why we think or act the way we do, regarding a particular situation".

In Collins English Dictionary:
"Soul-searching is a long and careful examination of your thoughts and feelings, especially when you are trying to make a difficult moral decision or thinking about something that has gone wrong".

To me, I know the word soul searching has a lot more depth and breadth than how the words above collectively have created its meaning.

Instead of looking for more, I looked deeply into my own self and asked why I feel something is missing in each of these definitions. I knew by experience the word had a deeper meaning to me. I decided to come up with my own definition from my experience, as it mattered to me in numerous occasions in my life.

As a doctor, a coach, a mentor, a business owner, a mother, a wife, a daughter, a friend, a workmate, a relative, a cousin, I play many roles in my life. I took risks in my life which others viewed as 'foolish', I fell down numerous times when others felt that "clearly could have been avoided", I pursued avenues which others felt were "a waste of time". Apart from having a very supportive husband throughout all the ups and downs in my life, the biggest strength I had every single time was that I soul searched in each occasion.

Every time I felt I was losing control, 'it' was not what I wanted or "how should I do this", I soul searched. It comes easily to me now, almost like breathing if I'm not exaggerating, as I have put it to practice many times. I will not say the measures I have taken have always been correct, but I found out that I can live with the decisions I made. Soul searching helped me to look at my decisions and actions before I acted upon them and helped me make sure that they were not in conflict with my moral principles and value streams. In short, soul searching helped me to live peacefully during rough times. Here are some tips to help you when you need to do some soul searching and how to do it effectively.

1. **Recognizing depletion is the first step in soul retrieval:**

   When you are constantly being sent messages by your brain that something is not right, constant feelings of inadequacy, discomfort, feelings of getting out of control, exhaustion or disconnection, STOP and Take a break! Time is calling you to have a deep chat with your inner self for your existence.

   Back in 2016 I was in a prestigious organization having a highly paid career. But for a long time, I felt something was missing from my life, and deep exhaustion and disconnection were creeping into my life. One day, I decided that I needed a break and I took a holiday to a faraway location. Consciously, I had booked an appointment with myself for soul searching, which ended up with the decision to change my career. I needed a lot of undisturbed 'ME time', hence I choose a sea side location, one of my favourites, where I can sit for hours and hours at my own pace.

2. Analyse the situation against your values and principles

When I was looking at my previous situation of disconnection, I realized many things about myself. I heavily valued contribution to human kind and making a difference even in a small way. I have continuously felt that many of the people whom I associated with at work were lacking that drive and passion. They focused on short term goals, and as such were hindering our collective ability to make and "actual impact", a difference. And above all, I was also lacking in 'family time'. I realized that I had not been paying attention adequately, as I was constantly busy with meeting short-term deadlines in projects. I realised that I was not feeding into my values and moral principles. I needed a big change in my life.

3. Look deeper into your inner being, it has all its answers there.

In moments when you feel "most" vulnerable, I have always found that soul searching is the better option over any other option available to us. I truly believe no one knows yourself and your 'actual' feelings than your own self. If you dare to ask yourself the right questions, 'why am I feeling this way?', 'what is the true situation that makes me feel this way' and uncover the truth about your feelings, the rest is easy. Keep looking deeper and ask, 'what would help make things better? What should I do differently to feel differently?' These are great questions to explore the answers you have within yourself. At first when the answers start to emerge you may feel they are too scary or overwhelming, but I challenge you to continue to explore without cutting yourself mid-way or prematurely because you feel scared. Look at it positively, as you know the best answers are within yourself and you are involved in the process of uncovering them by yourself.

When I realised that I needed a career change, it was a scary thought, as I have been a trained professional in a certain area of work for years. Instead of cutting off my thought generation process, I decided to be a spectator sitting in a movie, and let the movie play to the end. At the end of the movie, I still had the same thought.

4.   **Let it sink in. It takes time and that's fine.**

When I came back home, I felt revived and happy though I was not certain about the ultimate decision. I started to explore more, read, talk to people and ask questions, thinking it may be a sign the universe has given me.

Recently I met a coaching client of mine with whom I did voluntary sessions sometime back. When she came to me, she kept saying that she hated the psychiatric medicines she was on, as they made her feel drowsy. We did a few coaching sessions and I saw her slowly transitioning at her own pace. Recently she underwent a considerable emotional trauma associated with her family, but when I saw her again, she told me: 'I know today I can stand on my feet because of you'. I would never have known that I have the power to touch lives in such a significant way, would I have discarded the calling after my soul searching without further exploring.

5.   **Take initiative, once you have decided.**

Don't hesitate to take action to reach your goals, once you have clearly decided the course of following your soul searching. Only you can change the situation that you are in, no one else can do that for you. The advantage of reaching decisions through soul searching is that you'll always feel comfortable with the decisions taken as they agree with your inner principles, and they were your decisions. While I had great support from many individuals as I decided to move on, I knew all actions were to be initiated predominately by myself.

Looking back, it was a huge jump, but once it was broken down into smaller steps, the overwhelming feeling was gone and the excitement was growing inside me. Today, I know that if I had to go through the same process once more, I wouldn't change a thing. That confidence that I feel is because of the soul searching that I did prior to listening to others.

Coming back to the definition of the soul searching, to me it should be:
'It's a process of long and careful self-analysis of how one

reacts to a particular situation, considerate of one's values and moral principles, and finding solutions hidden deep inside of one's inner being, which gives confidence to move on to living the best life one deserves'.

I truly believe soul searching will not only help you come to terms with difficult situations, but it also helps you to live the best life you deserve.

Happy Soul Searching!

Charuni Senanayake
© 2018 Dr Charuni Senanayake

Life Coach,
Executive Coach
 and
Coach Trainer

Tools, Models, Techniques

An
Introduction

As with all development or growth, a range of tools, techniques, and models is available for each person to use either for themselves or to help and support other people.

Although there are no true definitions and in the personal and professional industries the terms 'tools' and 'techniques' are often used interchangeably, the professionals in these industries often use 'tools' to generally mean the 'instrument' to be used, and 'techniques' is all about the way in which the tools are used.

In some ways the 'techniques' are more important than the actual 'tools' that are used. Individuals coming into the personal and professional development world will use Role Models to model their use of the 'tools' and build up their own experience in their 'techniques'.

Coach training explains that each individual's own behaviour, which is based upon their values and beliefs, determine how each person makes their own decisions. Using an industry proven tool with the correct techniques will aid transformation, behavioural changes, and help individuals take steps into the unknown.

This issue will highlight probably the top two 'coaching' tools, and over the future issues we'll discuss these in more detail as well as continue through the known and unknown range of tools.

LISTENING

A skill that we all think we have, but do we? There is a lot more to listen than simply sitting there hearing the words. Are you listening while thinking about yourself in your response? Are you listening while thinking about the person who is talking and the type of response you'll give them? Are you listening while thinking about what the person talking needs in your response to them? Are you listening and not thinking about the type of response you'll give?

Listening is truly the most important skill that we can use in communication, especially when you are helping someone grow and develop. Listening at the right level (more on this in later articles) demonstrates a respect for the person talking; builds a level of trust and then intimacy. Coaches who are skilful listeners will learn a huge amount about their clients, the person they are talking to; often things that have not been shared with anyone else.

QUESTIONING

To truly hear what is being said effective questioning is crucial. A coach who is skilful at asking questions will elicit all the information that the person talking needs to hear before making their decision. Effective questioning will provide an in-depth and valuable level of information, sometimes new and not known, and at other times clarifying and reflecting. The information that the client or talker can share when the question is the right question sometimes brings a level of emotion that highlights how important the discovery, through the effective questioning, is.

More on the different types of questioning in future articles.

Take time out and share with us the tools and techniques you have found successful.

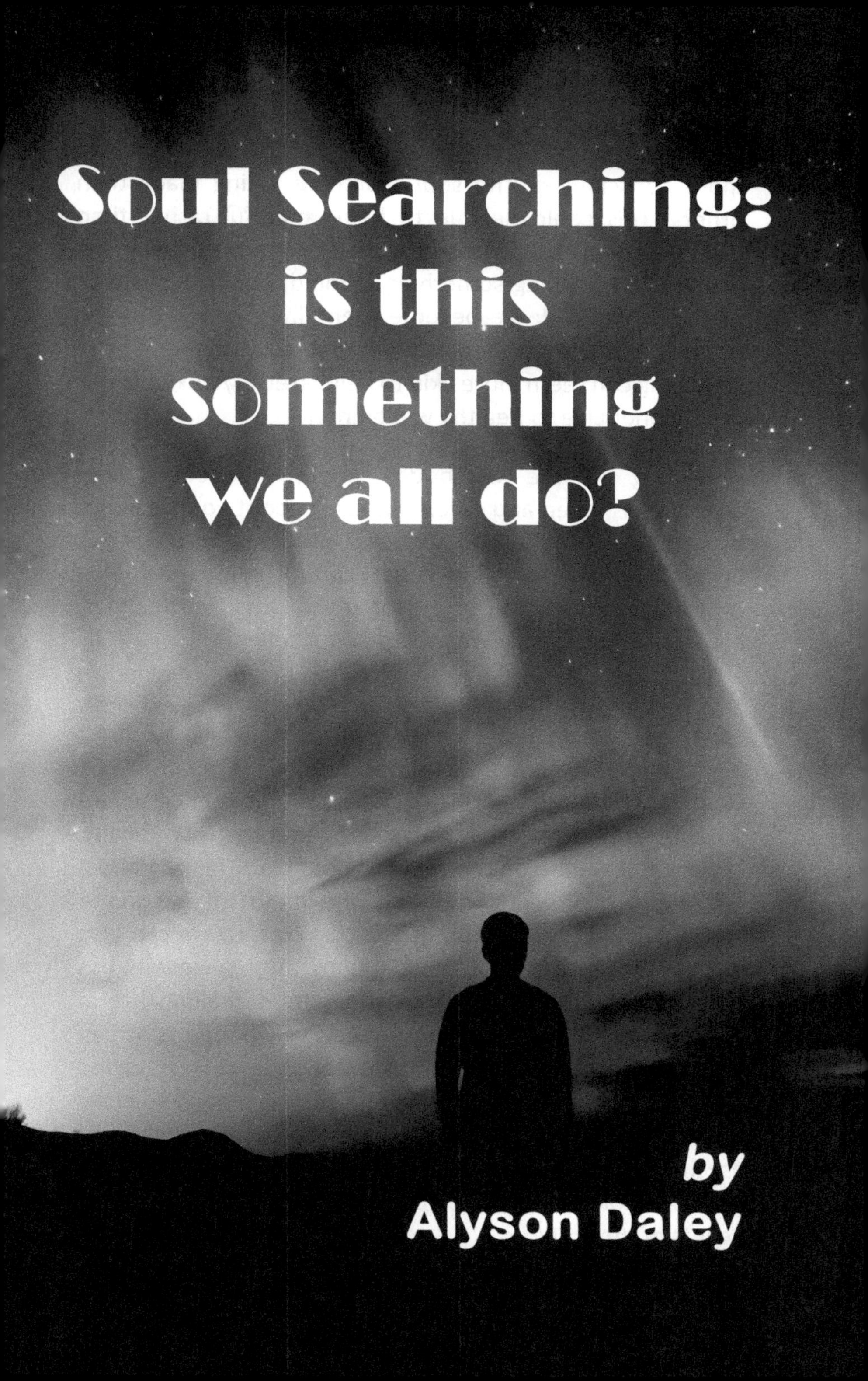
Soul Searching:
is this
something
we all do?
by
Alyson Daley

We definitely do, some more than others, and some are more conscious of the soul searching taking place than others. This could be due to being mindful rather than having a mind full. Mindful, actively attentive, aware & deliberately keeping something in mind; polar opposite of what is mind *full;* we become mentally absent from the present moment. When we are not fully present, soul searching can seem more akin to being fretful / anxious; this is not conducive to healthy wellbeing.

According to the Cambridge English dictionary soul searching is 'deep and careful thought about your feelings, especially in relation to a moral problem or decision'. Encarta dictionary define it as: 'careful consideration; a thorough examination of personal thoughts and feelings, especially when faced with a difficult problem'.

We are all faced with personal thoughts and feelings, especially when we encounter a problem, which for most parts happen on a daily basis; some are more complex / challenging than others. Some can leave us reeling where we stagger backwards, not suggesting that this is physically, however, if we are on our feet it is possible. This can affect our mental health, our wellbeing, and in turn impact on our soul searching experience. In addition to this, we can also be left wondering about our actions after an event has occurred, especially when our thoughts & feelings are in direct contrast to our actions. When this happens, it can have such an impact on our wellbeing; this is called cognitive dissonance, this is where there is a contradictory mental state, and it has been described as 'a state of psychological conflict or anxiety resulting from a contradiction between a person's simultaneously held beliefs or attitudes'.

This implies, and accurately so, that we can be hesitant to be our true selves, sometimes so much so that we forget who we truly are and at times lose who we are; this is why soul searching is vital, to feel that connection with ourselves again. If you can take some time out, search your soul and ask yourself why, where does this fear come from? Would you agree that this fear is based on our need or search to be accepted? When we conduct our lives; we are in our human form, for most parts of that, we conduct ourselves in order to fit the need of others, a sense of belonging, and this is completely natural. However, when we search our soul at the same time of actively being mindful, we reconnect with ourselves our inner self; this is a powerful & positive skill to possess.

Let me ask you a few questions:

What if we were our real true authentic selves?

What would happen if were?

What would that look like?

What would it feel like?

When we search our soul, we find the answers, we know. I am not suggesting that we have to be rebellious by being authentic, I mean being true to whom you are. Speaking & acting from the heart never fails.

Search your soul, and you'll have the answers and your emotional & psychological self will thank you for it.

Some lyrics for you:

Soul searching is what we do,
Soul searching is who we are
Soul searching is innate in us
Soul searching is positive
*   & is also negative*
We want answers
We want them now
We don't want to wait around for them
Yet soul searching is moments in time;
*   they come in spiral form*
Up then down

Back up then up even
*   further then slide back down*
An all-encompassing embrace
*   of toing & froing*

What are we soul searching for?
Our voice

That companion
That job
That pay rise
That holiday
The meaning of life

What is the meaning of life?
It's within us
Yet seems a trillion miles away
It's unreachable
It's not in our lifetime

What if it was, just for one minute

For one second
What would it look like?
Could you see it
Could you grasp it
Could you taste it
As though it was real?
Who knows, that's up to you
It's your reality
That's the joy in all of this
search your soul

It's all about you xoxox

Alyson Daley
© 2018 Alyson Daley

Lecturer in Psychology (University of Huddersfield and Bradford College), Huddersfield Change Project volunteer, Mental Health Practitioner, and Energy Mover

Take Action!

Exercise your Soul!

In recent years a lot of focus has been put on physical exercise, but not as much time is allocated to focusing on our souls. Our souls are our inner most being, and when we are not focusing on or recognising what they need; we aren't giving ourselves the same level of exercise that we more frequently give our physical bodies.

In the same way as you would exercise your physical body to increase your strength, this episode of Amarantine gives you the opportunity to exercise your soul; which will increase your feeling of peace, kindness, and joy in your world and the physical world around you.

The following exercises are scientifically proven in research, and give you the time and opportunity to connect with your soul. In doing so, you will also improve your physical and spiritual health and happiness.

1.   **Feel gratitude.**
      At least once a day you should give thanks. You can do this either by writing in a gratitude journal or by yourself in a quiet moment before you go to bed, whisper your thanks. You can give thanks for the food you have eaten during the day, for being alive, for the drinks you have drunk during the day, for the family and friends in your circle, the colleagues in your life, the good things that happened, and the lessons that you learnt.

2.   **Be generous.**
      Being generous doesn't mean spending money. You can be generous with your time, or by demonstrating your concerns about and showing your considerations for other people.   Being

generous in some ways goes hand-in-hand with feeling gratitude. Often when you demonstrate your gratitude you will become more generous in your thoughts, your time, and your feelings about others.

3. **Forgive.**
    This is one of the most powerful exercises for the soul that you can do.
    Forgive yourself!
    Forgive others!
    Let go of all the hurt, the pain, the anger, the hurt, the sorrow, and the resentment. As you let go of these feelings, consciously forgive yourself or others. As you let go, you'll begin to experience transformation.

4. **Meditate.**
    Meditation simply means a quiet time when you can empty your mind, relax your body, and mind. Find yourself a quiet time with no disturbances and focus on one thing; for example, your breathing, the waves hitting the beach, or specific piece of music. Let your mind focus on that one thing and stop all other thoughts. If you find other thoughts coming in as you sit there, consciously let it go. If you haven't meditated before; it does become easier the more you meditate.

5. **Walk in nature.**
    It is often said that you can communicate with nature, and that you can connect to your inner self – your soul. As you walk through nature become aware of the colours, the sounds, and the smells. As other thoughts come into your mind, consciously let

them go. Focus on what is around you.

6. **Sit in nature**.
   This is a combination of meditation and walking in nature, when you are sitting quietly and let nature absorb your troubles, your concerns, and your questions. Consciously put your thoughts into the ground, place fertiliser around your thoughts, and let nature nurture them. Once you have safely placed your thoughts into the ground, express your gratitude (see point 1 above).

7. **Pay attention.**
   Whether you realise it or not, your mind is processing around 75,000 thousand thoughts a day – things someone else has said, to-do lists, shopping lists, worries, and the list goes on. One of the steps when taking action to connect with your soul, gives you the opportunity to start to pay attention to what you are (1) hearing, (2) feeling, (3) hearing in your inner most soul; your heart. Stop watching so much television. Switch your mobile off. Put your book down. Look around you. Notice where you are. Paying attention is made easier with the use of a journal. Simply follow the next step.

8. **Write.**
   There are many places you can write, but if you want to write your own inner most secret thoughts, we suggest that you write a journal. A journal means you can write anything and everything. You can write anything and in any format. Bullet points. Notes. Poems. Sentences. Paragraphs. Chapters.
   Write down your gratitudes. Write down your

generosities. Write down what your forgive yourself for. Write down what you forgive others for. Write down anything you remember as part of your meditations. Write down your nature experiences. Write down anything about all your experiences when you start to pay attention. Write down anything and everything.

9. **Question.**

Question everything. Question yourself. What is stopping you from knowing what is in your soul? What is stopping you from living your dream? What is stopping you from changing the way things are today? What is the reason you let things happen? What is the reason you don't say 'no'?

Ask the question and then let your soul provide you with the answer. Often we stop ourselves from hearing the true answer from our soul because we are thinking about each question logically. It's often worthwhile asking these questions when you are meditating, having a quiet moment, or even being in nature. Write down the answers as you hear them – don't interpret what you hear.

10. **Dream.**

When you are sitting or walking through nature, ask yourself questions like 'what would a completely happy and joyful life look and feel like'? Now allow yourself to dream. Do you dream at night? Do you remember your dreams? Write down your dreams. As you finish writing down your dream, add '... and I allow this dream to come true.'

11.   **Sing.**

It is said that music is 'the most accessible and most researched medium of art and healing'. When you sing you are exercising your whole inner body. You are focusing on your internal you. You are masking all those other thoughts, more often than not calming your mind and your body while you are singing. You can do one, more or all of the points above; but if you select to do none of them right now think of a song which has meaning to you and sing it at the top of your voice.

It's all in the Numbers

Numbers

Numerology Series

Introduction

by

Loren Schmal

For anyone who is interested, curious or even a true believer, the basic definition of numerology is the universal language of numbers. By breaking down the patterns of the universe into numbers, we are able to uncover information about the world as a whole, as well as every individual. Numerology is the science of numbers, but it only involves simple mathematics.

It's more about the personalities of each number, and how each numbers' traits alter the course of your life depending on where they appear in your personal Numerology - if they appear at all. Numerology is a tool used to investigate our own very being, and to bring light our highest potential on the physical, emotional, mental and spiritual planes. Numerology tells of our potential destiny, our natural talents and helps us gain a better understanding of ourselves and others. It shows us the pathway we need to take in our lives to fulfill this potential, and also, tells us one of the many reasons why each one has different traits and characteristics. Numbers have been in existence since the beginning of time and predates all Alphabets.

Each number has a different vibration, and can therefore give us a better understanding of one's pathway, and the circumstances which surround our life. It can direct one to the career best suited to each person, and gives us the opportunity to be more aware of the talents we have and of the pathways we choose to utilize them. It also tells us of the compatibility we have with another, especially who would be most compatible as a partner for you. It tells you how you may best help your family and friends, due to the numbers which control their lives.

Each number is influenced by a different planet in our Solar

System. Each letter of the alphabet vibrates to a given number, 1 – 9, which is also the span of our life cycles. The numbers under which we were born, plus the numbers in our names, are the tools that we are given in order that we may accomplish our mission in life, and enable us to work through all our Karmic Lessons. The Vibratory Power of each number affects us in both Positive and Negative ways.

HOW TO WORK OUT
YOUR OWN NUMEROLOGY

The symbolic meanings that surround the nine whole numbers are the centre of Numerological divination. Numbers are also keyed to letters of the alphabet, so words and names, as well as dates of birth, can be analysed.

Numerology in
Relation to the Alphabet

Each letter of the alphabet is represented by a number between 1 and 9.

1	–	A	J	S
2	–	B	K	T
3	–	C	L	U
4	–	D	M	V
5	–	E	N	W
6	–	F	O	X
7	–	G	P	Y
8	–	H	Q	Z
9	–	I	R	

NAME NUMEROLOGY

The First Name is our 'Foundation in Life'.

To find the total Numerological vibration of your name, translate the letters of your name into the numbers as listed above, and add those number together. Then, break down the result in separate numbers, which you add up again, until you have reduced it to a single digit number. This number is known as your Name Ruling Number.

As an example, let's take the name Chantel. This name translates to C=3, H=8, A=1, N=5, T=2, E=5, L=3.

When we add those numbers (3+8+1+5+2+5+3) we get to 27.

As this is a double digit, which we still need to reduce to 1 digit, we add the numbers of this result.

So: 2+7=9.

The Name Ruling Number for the name Chantel is therefore 9.

DATE OF BIRTH NUMEROLOGY

DAY NUMBER

Your Day Number is the energy which influences who you are and all that you do in your life, on a daily basis. It tells of what makes you respond and act as you do, and is an indication of what type of life you should lead in order to be successful in all that you undertake in this lifetime.

Your Day Number is the day of your birth.

Using as an example the 26th of September 1967, the Day Number is 26 = 2 + 6 = 8.

8 is the Day Number.

DESTINY NUMBER

The destiny number is one of the most important numbers on your chart. It is the ruling force that describes what you must do/learn, in order to operate harmoniously with your environment and how you can get the most out of your present life. It shows the direction you must take, representing the only opportunities for success that will be made available to you.

To analyse and interpret your 'Destiny Number', simply use the formula of reducing your entire date of birth to a single digit.

For example, the 'Destiny Number' for a person with the date of birth of the 26th of September 1967 is
2+6+0+9+1+9+6+7 = 40,
4+0 = 4.

PERSONAL YEAR

The Personal Year Number is the energy by which you will live your life from your birthday of this year, until your birthday of next year. This is the vibration that will influence all that you do throughout that period.

The Personal Year energy is present from birthday to birthday. To work out your Personal Year Number, take the Day and Month Numbers and add them to the Year Number.

For example, the Personal Year Number in 2018 for someone with the date of birth 26/09/1967 would be Number 1. Add the day and month numbers to the year number (2018)
2+6+0+9+2+0+1+8 = 28:
2 + 8 = 10:
1+0=1, making 1 the Personal Year Number.

Loren Schmal
© 2018 Loren Schmal

Founder of CyberPA

It's all in the Numbers

Numbers

Numerology Series

7

by

Loren Schmal

As this issue of Amarantine is about Soul Searching, I thought it relevant to give the numerological meaning of the words "Soul Searching" and its significant numbers. Soul Searching relates to the number 7.

Number 7 resonates with the vibrations and energies of the 'Collective Consciousness', faith and spirituality, spiritual awakening and awareness, spiritual enlightenment, spiritual development, mysticism, intuition and inner-knowing, inner-wisdom, psychic abilities, the esoteric, inner-selves, deep contemplation, introspection, eccentric, religion, thoughtfulness, understanding of others, natural healer and healing, secrets, myth, ritual, peace, poise, emotions and feelings, inner-strength, endurance and perseverance, persistence of purpose, the ability to bear hardships, quick-wit, the loner, solitary, isolation, long-sighted, the non-conformist, independence and individualism, intentions, manifesting and manifestation in time and space and good fortune.

Number 7 also relates to the attributes of mental analysis, philosophy and philosophical, technicality, scientific research, science, alchemy, genius, a keen mind, specialising and the specialist, the inventor, determination, the written word, logic, understanding, knowledge, discernment and discerning, knowledge seeking, study, education and learning, writing and the writer, evolution, stability, the ability to set limits, completion, refinement, stoicism, silence, perfection, chastity, dignity, ascetic, rigor, ahead of the times.

7 is a 'magical' vibration and is the number of the occultist and the esoteric. 7's are secretive, mysterious, stand-offish, intuitive and introspective. An unworldly attitude means

most 7's need to be 'protected'. The 7 vibration represents rest, contemplation, spirituality, sensitivity, sympathy and mastery. 7 is a number of the 'mind'.

The 7 energy has very strong psychic tendencies and are natural healers with a core of inner-strength. 7 is the sacred spiritual number – 'the energy of the mystics'. They are known to be quick-witted, sometimes with a dry sense of humour.

Number 7 is considered a masculine energy as well as an introvert. The related planet is Mercury and it is related to the star sign Libra. The associated Tarot card is The Chariot.

The 7 vibration represents a special function of human life and indicates the amount of learning one must amass in the form of personal experiences known as 'sacrifices'.

The first cycle of 7 deals with the physical process. The second cycle from ages 7 to 14 is marked by the development of feelings and emotions. The third cycle from ages 14 to 21 focuses on the spiritual energy. This is when the 'light of spirit' begins to dawn into a maturing consciousness.

I'm sure that you'll agree that, given all of the above, the number 7 perfectly aligns with "Soul Searching", as it symbolizes humanity's deep inner-need to find depth, meaning and spiritual connection. When the needs of food, self-expression, material and domestic achievements have been met, the 7 energy turns to the deeper levels of life - to learn, to educate ourselves and to find purpose. The 7 vibration must continue studying the quest of why they are here. 7 asks the bigger questions!

What does it mean if you find a Number 7 In your own numbers?

In our Introduction to Numerology we've explained how you can calculate your own numbers. Have any of your numbers turned out to be a 7? If yes, then please find below an explanation as to what this means.

COLOURS associated with number 7

Grey and **Purple** are colours that Number 7's will feel comfortable with. They are calm and soothing colours that reflect the desire of number 7's to blend in. Bold colours should be avoided by number 7's.

Number 7 LIFE CHALLENGES

Number 7 has a great deal of trouble dealing with emotions and they may feel as if they have to repress their feelings in order to survive. As a child this can lead to introversion, obsessiveness and a complete retreat from reality.

As an adult they may suffer from chronically negative thoughts and express them through constant complaining or criticism of others. Many 7's are hypochondriacs or manifest disease as a result of suppressed anger or grief.

7 as a DAY NUMBER

Spiritual, intuitive and sensitive, you hate noise, disturbances and hustle and bustle. You are an expert on human nature and love learning new skills. Life though often throws you many obstacles to overcome. People with the energy of the 7 are quite often loners and their mission in life is to learn to have faith, always.

The 7 Day person often ends up teaching others more than they may learn themselves, need solitude and their own space, and can often find it a little difficult 'fitting in'. From their early 20's, 7 Day people are well aware and reach their special purpose and have natural healing abilities.

The 7 Day individual has great wisdom with strong intuition, clairvoyance and psychic abilities. 7 is never satisfied until they can link the known with the unknown, and this leads to a great deal of research, analysis and investigation. The 7 energy is the perfectionist and the thinker and they are urged to investigate the deeper things in life. Knowledge and wisdom are their goals and their quick intelligence and inquiring mind leads them to investigate many areas.

7s have a love of natural beauty such as flowers, plants, oceans, seas and lakes etc. 7's have an air of mystery about them, and they do not want anyone to know too much about them, so they often come off as aloof and withdrawn. It is difficult to figure out what they are thinking and feeling at any given moment as they keep to themselves and are quite introspective. 7's can shut themselves off and make you feel that they are not remotely interested in what you are doing or saying – but in reality, they are the ultimate observers and they don't miss a trick.

The 7 is an investigator, an inventor and this energy must have solitude in which to be able to hear their inner-voice. 7's tend to be 'different', eccentric, or loners, and are very discriminating in all areas. 7 people demand a lot of themselves and others due to their extremely high standards. These people need to spend a lot of time on their own to reflect, meditate and work. They are very independent and introspective, and do not always like to join in with others. They often prefer to remain behind the scenes, where they can freely roam.

The calm, serene and quiet presence of the 7 energy keeps these people in the background and it would be easy for them to become a recluse. They do not like to mix with the crowd and can give off the appearance of being distant and aloof. Many number 7's build a wall of protective reserve around themselves as they do not want their world filled with lots of people, but prefer a few close, intimate associations who are of their choosing.

The finer things in life are important to the 7 vibration, and they are discriminating about their wants and needs. They prefer the best and will be selective of home, environment, possessions and quality of relationships. They are selective in diet, food and habits, and with self-control they adhere to their own values of correct eating and nutrition in general.

Trips to the ocean and nature adventures are important to regenerate the 7 vibration as the peaceful surrounds of nature give 7 people the opportunity to be in touch with the mystical side of their lives. 7's are interested in phenomena, the unexplainable, the supernatural and the spiritual aspects of life.

The number 7 person has an outstanding ability to heal people on the spiritual, emotional and physical levels. In return, they need the love and appreciation of those around them. They are able to intuitively tune into the emotions and needs of others.

The 7 energy fears failing to achieve by their own standards and making mistakes.

7 as a DESTINY number

Positive Characteristics:

People born with 7 as their Destiny or Life Path Number are sensitive and compassionate. They have a natural wisdom and ability to see to the truth of matters.

The 7 energy feels the need to investigate all things themselves so that they are able to come to their own decisions and value systems. They are the thinker, the dreamer and philosopher who can leave the world behind and go into the world of creative imagination. They search for their own belief system.

The mental ability and sensitivity of the 7 person gives them the opportunity to develop their intuitive, clairvoyant and psychic gifts. The 7 is aware of the spiritual side of life and knows that without turning into their inner resources, their outer world is not at peace. The deeper they delve, the more they learn to trust their intuition and to have faith and trust, the more they will reach the higher levels of their wisdom.

Once people get to know a Number 7 they will find an exceptional person who is able to offer warmth, sympathy and understanding. Number 7s take their time to consider problems and weigh up the pros and cons of any given situation before coming to their conclusion. Number 7

Destiny people are adaptable and adjust easily to change. This tends to be because they are generally happy within themselves.

The Destiny of 7 is to use the mind on the mystical side of life and to develop the wisdom of the spiritual aspects of life. 7's are never satisfied until they can

link the known with the unknown and this leads to a great deal of investigation, research and analysis.

The Number 7 transcends the barriers of time and space and brings you in touch with the world of the mystic and clairvoyant. On a lower plane of manifestation, it gives a confused sense of timing and a dislike of restrictions.

The **challenge** for 7's is to overcome their obstacles, particularly bad relationship experiences.

Their **purpose** is to experience spiritual growth.

Negative Characteristics:

Number 7's often lack confidence in their abilities and do not like to draw attention to themselves, and as a result their talents often go unnoticed. As a result of their lack of confidence many number 7's find it difficult to communicate effectively with other people and can come across as being vague.

There is a tendency for number 7's to be dreamers as they spend so much of their time immersed in their own thoughts. They should be wary of becoming cut off from the outside world and should make the effort to socialize with their friends.

A sign that a number 7 has strayed completely off of his or her life path is a complete withdrawal from society.

Number 7 as a PERSONAL YEAR

Even if you have a reputation of an extrovert, a year 7 is likely to put you in the mood to be alone. You may feel like pursuing your interests, travelling or finding a way to escape from business pressures. A 7 Personal Year is like a cocooning stage for the psyche, in which you analyse, reflect and try to shed any behaviours, relationships or patterns that may be preventing your personal growth. Being alone with nature makes a positive difference in your state of mind.

The 7 Personal Year favours any kind of self-improvement, including surgical operations, seeking counselling or therapy or seeking higher education. The 7 Personal Year is a year to enrich your spiritual side. The important questions, 'Who am I? What am I? Why am I here and what is my purpose?' are appropriate areas to look into this year.

This is a year of spiritual, rather than personal, progress and changes. There can be many changes within, which can deeply affect our emotions, forcing one to think more carefully about the consequences of our thought and actions. Changes during this year will make one more aware of where their personal strengths lie. It is a year of learning and this can only occur through personal experience, which to many, means sacrifice.

Meditation and yoga would be a good thing to take up in this cycle. Trust your intuition. When we fail to accept our higher guidance, and choose to live only in the material world, we can open ourselves up to material losses in love and health, or both. It is especially important to avoid any large-scale business dealings or financial investments during this year.

The 7 Personal Year is a year of consolidation. This is somewhat of a sabbatical time. Much is gained through reflection and personal refinement. You may want to ask yourself some important questions like what your **life purpose** is and what you want your life to be like. It is a time for seeking a deeper understanding into your inner nature. Solitude is often needed in order to quiet your mind and get in touch with what really matters to you.

Number 7 CAREER OPPORTUNITIES

The 7 energy has many diverse talents and would do well in the fields of the researcher, analyst, the law, criminal detective, investigative work, professor, consultant, spiritual careers, Minister, astrologer, numerologist, analyst, earth/maritime occupations, occultist, healer, writer, actor, comedian, the medical profession, spiritual careers, interests in the past, e.g. history, antiques, archaeology, art. All these things require a good education.

Number 7 in CAREER

Intuitive, quick-witted and persuasive, 7's make a brilliant lawyer, comedian or debater. 7's intellectual and studious personalities often pursue advanced academic careers. As they love to absorb information, they usually require a great deal of private time to cultivate their knowledge. These reserved and analytical deep-thinkers make great mathematicians, engineers, inventors, scientists and doctors.

Number 7's are not driven by ambition and have no desire for excessive material wealth. They are hard-working and committed individuals, but they must feel that their hard work benefits the world at large, and not just themselves. For this reason, number 7's are often found working in voluntary organizations and the caring professions. For some Number 7's their desire for escapism could be met by a career in the travel industry as the opportunity to visit far-off places, combined with ensuring that others enjoy their holiday, can be a very rewarding combination.

Honesty and independence are admirable qualities found in number 7's, but these can cause difficulties in some working environments. Number 7's will never let a dishonest act or an act that offends their sense of integrity go unchallenged. This can lead to number 7's challenging their employers and creating an unwanted scene. It is important for number 7's to accept that there are some professions that require a certain amount of flexibility and that they may not be suited to careers in such areas of work. If they do choose a career in one of these professions, number 7's will need to refrain from challenging their employers if they wish to succeed.

Loren Schmal
© 2018 Loren Schmal

Founder of CyberPA

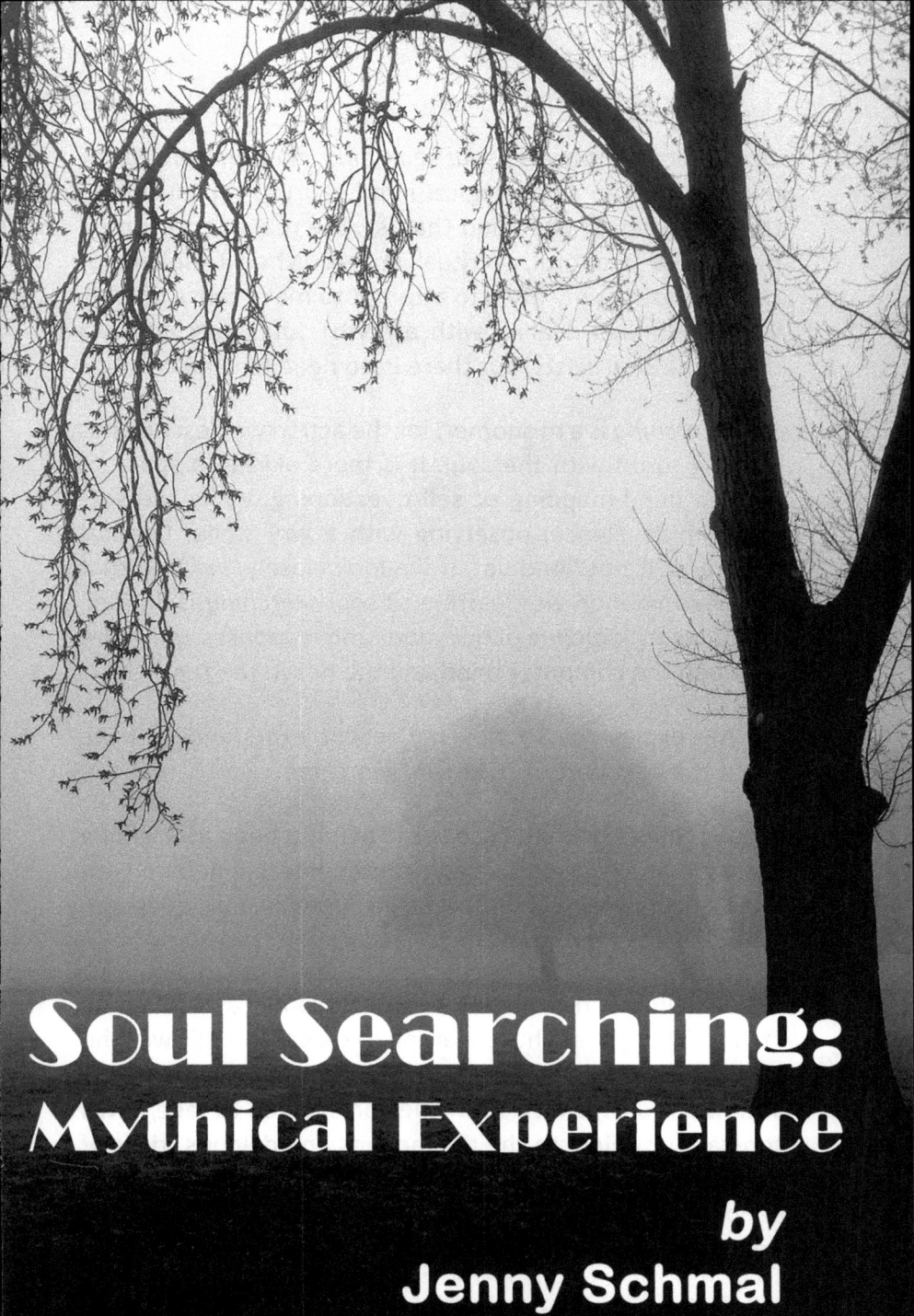

Soul Searching:
Mythical Experience

by
Jenny Schmal

That evocative phrase, *soul searching,* had enchanted my mind, but, even as my logical mind courted the illusion of the expression, " the mind that is", the real me presented me with a beautiful, spiritual image. When I looked for clarity, allowing my mind to attempt to make sense of it all, I realised I was dealing with a myth! *Soul searching* is a myth. The soul exists, but there is no need to search for it.

Soul searching is a misnomer, for the action we describe has nothing to do with the soul. It is more akin to a space of intense mind-mapping or self-questioning, while the soul looks on in silence, observing with a wry smile. Comical picture, is it not? And yet, if we look closely, we find that the phenomenon we describe as *soul searching* is, in fact, the on-going dialogue of questions and responses which fire between the computer mind and the heart, the real self.

Let me explain by sharing my recent experience. I have spent the best part of 2017 *soul searching.*

When I reflect on that, I can see that it has been a year-long excursion into my mind, a convoluted internal debate with myself concerning the recurring, persistent question: "Should I write a book?"

The conclusion has always been the same; a resounding "Yes!" although, as I have learned to recognise, this was the reply of my heart. Although I knew that my heart was my authentic voice, which *knew* the correct step to take, I was constantly subject to the distractions and devious tricks of the mind. Looking back, I understand that my subconscious mind was in turmoil, frantically searching for ways to sabotage publication. Why?

In hindsight, it is clear: Something magical happens when

you first see your book in print - you change! You are now a published author and, as new channels of communication open up and unexpected opportunities present themselves, you become a different person.

That was the worst fear of the subconscious mind. Its subtle doubts and lies were all designed to keep me where I was – safe. Yes, of course it would allow me to declare my intention to publish. It would even let me write a few chapters, but, whenever it seemed that I might be close to formulating the finished article and initiating massive change, it would intervene with its best efforts to halt progress.

As my mind challenged my heart with a myriad of reasons why it could not be done – or, at least, why it should be put off until another day – the soul sighed softly at the dialogue between the two voices.

Although my heart, the speaker of the soul, knew what message I had to bring forth, my mind presented me with a myriad of reasons to prevent it from happening. Aside from the practical considerations of finding an editor, a formatter and a publisher who would take me on, the greatest struggle – and the most effective weapon in the armoury of my mind - was self-doubt; the fear that I would not be able to please everyone.

What subject matter should be included?

Was the list of subjects too long or too short?

What register of language and tone would engage readers or alienate them?

Was the content too radical or not radical enough?

Would it appeal to this person and put someone else off?

Would it really offer life-changing value to the reader?

In short, the mind knows our Achilles heel; that there will always be someone who knows something that we do not. It is our fear of not being good enough, that stops us from delivering the message we were born to share.

No human being knows the whole picture. In this Internet Age, each of us has access to the collective knowledge of millennia of human thought. So why write a book? Is there anything new left to say? There may be nothing new under the sun, but that does not give us a 'get out' clause to avoid our individual responsibility to deliver our unique message to those who are waiting for it.

Perfectionism is the last ditch attempt of the mind to prevent us from taking action, and keep us safe and stop our light from shining brightly to be seen by those who are looking for us. *Perfectionism* requires that our work must appeal to everyone in order to be commercially viable and to never receive a word of criticism. *Perfectionism* demands that we be all things to all men. In short, this is the mind's trump card; it knows that *perfectionism* is a cast-iron guarantee that it will never get done!

In order to circumvent the subtle strategies of my mind, I had to understand my objectives in publishing a book in the age of the World Wide Web and truly democratic access to book printing and distribution. A printed book is no longer a vanity project or the preserve of the academic, it is a platform from which we can reach those we have come to serve.

That knowledge is liberating and begs the mind to be silent.

The heart knows that you only have to reach those who are waiting for your message – not appeal to everyone and anyone. Your message is unique and your work, even though it may be similar to that of others, it is delivered by you, in your unique style.

The same book can serve diverse purposes for different people, and, on second or third readings, different perspectives for the same reader. Consider any book that has affected you sufficiently to return to it again and again. No matter how well you think you know the content, you will discover new insight every time you refer to it, because on your return, you are not the same person. As Heraclitus said: "No man ever steps in the same river twice, for it is not the same river and he is not the same man."

The purpose of publishing is service; it is direct delivery of the message you bring to the world. That message is unique to you, it is who you are. That is why it is important to know who you are writing for and why they are waiting for your message. The doubts of the mind arise when we consider all the people the book is *not* for. This is not a random universe. We are not simply shouting out to the world in the hope that someone will get us. We are here on a mission to connect with the ones who are here to receive our message.

Hoping that a book will be a commercial success is thinking by numbers. Knowing the group you are here to serve is an entirely different approach, and doesn't allow any headspace for the Ego to protect its precious reputation or need for universal approval. When you know your soul's purpose for your book, you can let go of going to get customers, and start going to give value for the unique, precious group of people waiting for you to serve them.

Now I know that here was no need for *soul searching*. My *soul* did not have to be *found*; it had been there all along, waiting for my mind to be silenced, so that it could be *allowed* to deliver its song. My mind did its best to prevent me from getting burnt, and yet my book emerged, like a phoenix rising from the embers of the heated debate.

My book is now completed, not by *soul searching*, but by silencing of the mind and allowing my heart to speak....

Jenny Schmal
© 2018 Jenny Schmal

Jenny Schmal ASC is available for private coaching, corporate events and can be booked as a motivational speaker.

QUESTION
EVERYTHING
Your Questions Answered

Dear Amarantine team,

I feel like I've hit a crossroad in my career. I drag myself to work every day and I feel drained by day end, so something needs to be changed. And I feel totally ready to make that next step, but the problem is that I have no clue whatsoever as to what that next step should be. I'm really afraid that I invest time and money in a new career, and then end up feeling the same a couple of years down the road. Can you help me figure out what I should do?

Teacher, Maryland VA, USA

Dear Teacher,

Many people have asked themselves the same questions at some point in their careers, and "soul searching" would be the answer. This issue of Amarantine provides you with tips, tools and techniques to get in touch with your inner most feelings to find the answers to these questions.

However, soul searching usually takes time, and the answers that you are looking for may not come overnight. Therefore, you may try and speed up the process by doing following exercises:

> Speak with your closest friends and family and ask them what they think would suite you best as a next career step and why. This may provide you with some valuable new insights and/or bring the most important things top of mind. Make sure to write down their suggestions and explanations.

Then, make a bullet point list of all you can think off that you like and dislike in your current role, and that you think you may or may not like for future roles. Try to keep this as much top level as you can, e.g. "(don't) like transferring knowledge" or "(don't) like working with kids" etc.

Start a new bullet point list and of all the things that you like/dislike doing in your private life. What energises you, and what not? (e.g. "(don't) like travel, (don't) like pets), (don't) like to read, (don't) like to watch TV, etc.)

Now that we have these 3 sheets of paper, let's see if we can combine all "likes" elements into your – yet non-existent and unnamed, and likely totally unrealistic - dream job. This may look something like: I would love to have a job in which I spend a lot of time reading, can speak French, work with animals, travel a lot". Make sure to list your likes in order of priority, starting with those which are a "must" for you, and working your way down to the "nice to haves".

Now that we've done the dreaming, it's time for a reality check. Extract 3-5 priority key words (e.g. reading, travel, French), enter these into a job search engine, and see what comes up. Are there any roles you like? Any that you don't? Review every one of them, and make sure to add any new findings to your lists.

And finally, start a new list as you're going through all these jobs to list any skills, knowledge, etc. that you may be short off to enter your new dream career.

This exercise should help you become clearer on what you want and what you can do to move into that direction.

And finally, picking up on your remark that you want to know for sure that you're making the right choice, please consider following. As we walk through life, it's perfectly natural to change course from time to time. Our priorities may change and life will likely throw us a few curve balls here and there too. This is no different for our careers, and chances are that in a few years from now you'll want to move on to the next thing.

Therefore, I'd like to suggest that you see your career as a journey rather than as a destination. You'll continue to learn more about your likes and dislikes as you experience new things, which will help bring you closer to your destination ('the perfect career") as you move on. You've just completed your inner road map to help guide you onto the best path for your next journey. If you check this road map from time to time, update it as and when required, and change course when you feel you want or need to, then I'm sure you'll be fine!

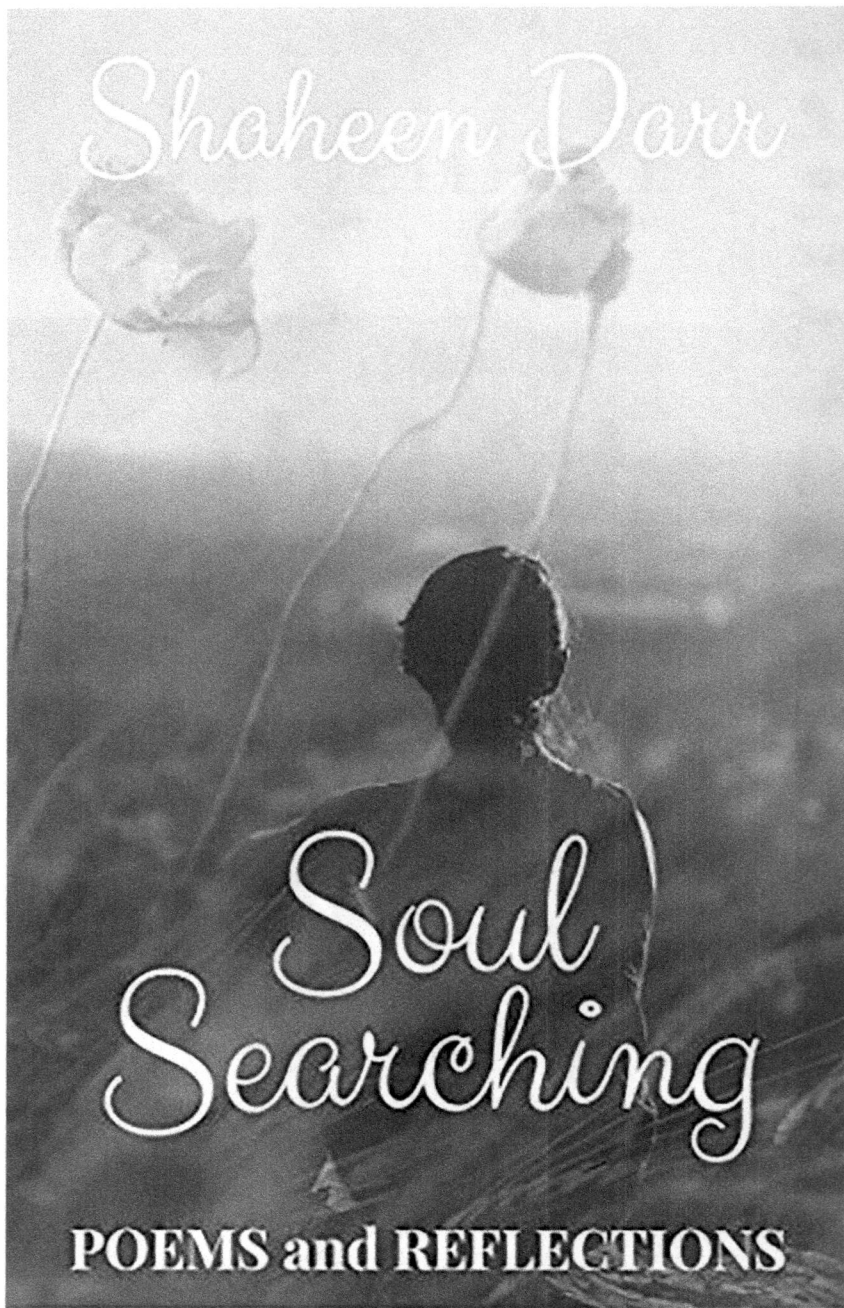

Welcome to your Personal and Professional Development with Amarantine

Amarantine supports your Personal and Professional Development through assessing, exploring, developing, and inspiring yourself to increase your self-awareness, self-knowledge, self-confidence, and self-esteem; to help you identify and develop your talents, skills, knowledge, competence, and experience to fulfil your personal aspirations in both your personal and professional life, to provide you with an enhanced lifestyle and improved quality of life as a result.

Whether you have a personal goal or a professional career goal, Amarantine will answer the questions you ask in an inspirational manner that helps you take the next step to achieve your own personal and professional aspirations.

Amarantine supports lifelong learning; which is achieved through both formal and informal learning processes. Formal learning is defined as education and training; whereas informal learning comes from coaching, mentoring, supervision, as well as things you experience, see, and hear in your everyday life.

Amarantine will inspire you to consciously learn and develop in all areas of your personal and professional life.

www.Amarantine.Life